DAN THUY'S
NEW LIFE IN AMERICA

DAN THUY'S
NEW LIFE IN AMERICA

Karen O'Connor

Lerner Publications Company / Minneapolis

Acknowledgments

The photographs in this book are by: pp. 2, 6, 7, 8, 10, 11, 12, 13, 14, 23, 24, 25, 26, 27, 29, 30, 31, 33, 35, 36, 37, 38, 39, Phillip C. Roullard; pp. 15, 20, 21, 22, UNHCR/A. Hollmann; p. 16, UNHCR/P. Deloche; pp. 18, 40, UNHCR/R. Manin.

Copyright © 1992 by Lerner Publications Company

Library of Congress Cataloging-in-Publication Data

O'Connor, Karen, 1938-
    Dan Thuy's New Life in America / Karen O'Connor
        p.   cm.
    Includes bibliographical references.
    Summary: Describes the experience of thirteen-year-old Dan Thuy Huynh and her family, recently come from Vietnam to live in San Diego, California, as they adapt to their life in a new country.
    ISBN 0-8225-2555-0
    1. Immigrants—California—San Diego—Juvenile literature.
2. Vietnamese—California—San Diego—Juvenile literature.
[1. Vietnamese Americans—California. 2. Immigrants—California.
3. United States—Emigration and immigration. 4. Huynh, Dan Thuy.]
I. Title.
JV6926.S25028   1992
325'.2597'09794985—dc20   91-28915
                                            CIP
                                            AC

Manufactured in the United States of America

1 2 3 4 5 6 7 8 9 10 01 00 99 98 97 96 95 94 93 92

Author's Note

I wish to thank Mr. Gu Thanh Huynh, his wife KimHong (Rose) Nguyen, and their daughters, Dan Thuy and Dan Tram, for allowing me to interview them for this book. I also extend special thanks to their relatives and sponsors, Sau (Sally) Thai and her daughter, Lee Thai, who graciously offered their hospitality and translating abilities during the interviewing process.

Large grocery stores and shopping malls are familiar sights to most Americans. But to 13-year-old Dan Thuy Huynh (pronounced *Dahn Twee Hween*), these are among the many surprising aspects of life in the United States. Fast food, movie theaters, computers, and the English language are also new to Dan Thuy and her family since they moved from Vietnam to San Diego, California, after spending three years in Thailand. They have lived in the United States just four months.

Vietnam, Dan Thuy's homeland, is a small country in Southeast Asia about the size of California. It is located south of China between the South China Sea on the east and Laos and Cambodia (also called Kampuchea) to the west.

The Huynh family
(left to right):
KimHong, Dan
Tram, Gu Thanh,
and Dan Thuy

Dan Thuy and her family are immigrants—people who have moved permanently from one country to another. In some ways, immigrants lead a double life. They are caught between the old culture and the new, between their native language and a new language, between friends in the old place and friends in the new.

Immigrants have populated the United States throughout its history. Since the early 17th century, more than 50 million people from countries all over the world have left their homelands for the religious, political, and economic freedom that America offers. Between 1904 and 1914 alone, nearly one million immigrants a year poured into the country. Following waves of European immigration early in the 20th century, many Asian and Hispanic people have moved to America in recent decades.

When the Huynhs arrived in the United States, they had an advantage that many immigrants do not have. Several members of their family had come to America during the mid-1970s, so aunts, uncles, cousins, and grandparents were there to greet them.

Many Vietnamese immigrants settle in Southern California because the warm, mild climate is similar to that of their native land. Some choose the area because they know other Vietnamese people there. The sight of people from their homeland helps immigrants feel that they belong.

This Sunday morning, Dan Thuy, her nine-year-old sister Dan Tram, and their parents, Gu Thanh and KimHong, visit relatives for brunch. Some members of the family leave their shoes at the door, following Vietnamese tradition. Others wear their shoes, preferring to follow the American custom.

Dan Thuy's uncle Nu is KimHong's brother. Nu and his wife Sau (known to her American friends as Sally) sponsored the Huynh family when they moved from Vietnam to the United States. A sponsor is a person or organization that agrees to help immigrants settle in the United States. The sponsor helps the immigrants find work and a place to live. Ten years ago, friends of Nu and Sau sponsored them and their five children when they came from Vietnam. Now it is Nu's turn to offer the same kind of help to his sister and her family.

The family gathers at Uncle Nu and Aunt Sally's house.

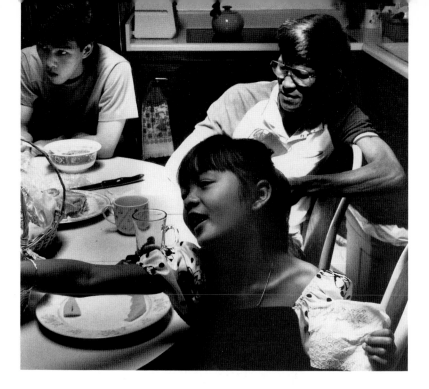

As everyone talks in Nu and Sau's sunny kitchen, some of the family members eat coffee cake and cinnamon rolls and drink coffee. Others prefer a Vietnamese dish—noodles and meat in a hot broth. Dan Thuy's cousin Lee slices a fresh mango using a traditional Vietnamese cutting tool.

Dan Thuy models her
Vietnamese dress.

Although Dan Thuy has only lived in the United States for a short time, she already wears clothing common to many American teenagers—leggings and an oversized T-shirt. She has not forgotten her traditional Vietnamese clothes, however. Before the visit is over, Dan Thuy models her red dress, matching long pants, and black patent leather shoes for her family. At one time, Vietnamese women wore this national dress every day, but now it is worn only on special occasions, such as Tet, the Vietnamese new year, or at weddings and other celebrations.

13

As they sit around the table, some family members speak English. Others speak Vietnamese. Some of the younger people even mix the two languages in one sentence.

Mastering a new language is not easy. Dan Thuy and her parents say they have much to learn. Dan Thuy's mother, KimHong, practices her English every day at her job in a manicure salon. But she still feels uncertain about her language skills.

Dan Thuy also worries about her English. "I have many fears," she says, "because English is my second language. I am afraid people will not understand what I say when I speak or write."

Gu Thanh is not working right now because of a back injury, so he uses his time to attend English classes. "I am really busy," he says with a wide smile. "I have to study, take care of my children, and find a job. There are many things to do."

Vietnamese refugees distribute food at a camp in Thailand.

The Huynh family first began to study English during the three years they lived in a refugee camp in Thailand. The United Nations defines refugees as "persons suffering persecution because of political opinion, membership in a particular social group, race, ethnicity, or religion." Refugees such as the Huynhs often leave their homeland because they fear death or imprisonment.

In 1975, after the Vietnam War, Communist soldiers from North Vietnam took over South Vietnam. In April the southern city of Saigon fell to North Vietnamese troops. The city became a mass of frightened people desperate to get out before they were killed or imprisoned. Men, women, and children clogged the streets and jammed the airport runways. They tried to leave by any means they could.

After this first wave of refugees fled Vietnam in 1975, the rate of people leaving the country slowed down. Then, during the 1980s, a second wave of refugees left the country because of difficult living conditions. Unfortunately, after 1975, planes were not available to fly people out of the country. The only way out was by boat. Citizens who fled Vietnam in this way—perhaps as many as 370,000 of them—came to be known as *boat people.*

The boat people tell many stories about the horrors they experienced on their journey to freedom. Some of the boats were so overcrowded they fell apart. Others sank in storms and rough waters. Still others set sail in bad weather and spent days drifting in fog and rain with little water and food for the passengers. In addition, pirates attacked the boats, robbing and sometimes even killing people.

Nonetheless, refugees continued to pour out of Vietnam. To remain there under the Communist regime could mean death, working for the state, or losing one's family ties. To those who could leave, risking death in a boat was better than life in a land of hatred.

Like so many others, the Huynhs fled the Communist regime and escaped Vietnam by boat. It was a very difficult time for Gu Thanh and his family. "When people escaped from Vietnam after the war, many were killed and a lot of women were raped by pirates," he says sadly. "I knew then it would be a most difficult thing to bring my family to the United States."

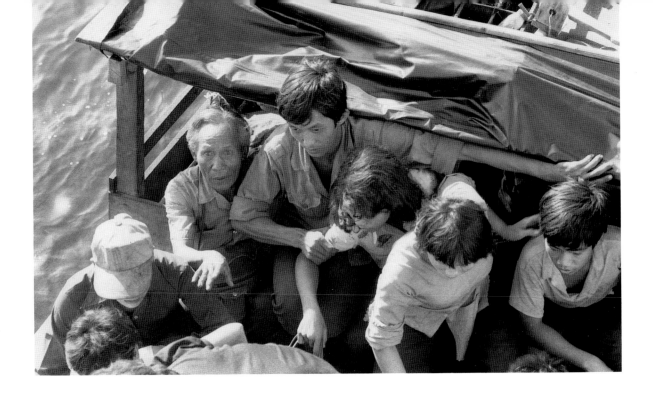

But Gu Thanh knew he must try to leave. "In my country," he says, "we have a saying, 'Freedom or death.'" He and his family sailed to Thailand, where they could stay in a refugee camp until it was possible to move to the United States.

"We were lucky," Gu Thanh reflects. "We were only on the sea for 24 hours. No one died and no women were raped." But he adds, "Before our trip, we had to stay in hiding in Kampuchea for one month. It was very hard. We were always nervous and afraid. We couldn't sleep and we had little food to eat."

The first refugee camps were put together quickly during the mid-1970s to provide a haven for the thousands of refugees who were fleeing Vietnam, Laos, and Cambodia (Kampuchea). Most of the early camps were overcrowded and dirty and lacked adequate food, clothing, and medicine.

During the 1980s, however, many of the camps improved under the management of the United Nations High Commissioner for Refugees. In addition, international relief organizations such as the Red Cross, CARE, World Vision International, and others provided medical care, clothing, food, and education.

Despite the changes, life in the refugee camp was still hard for the Huynh family. There were no luxuries and few jobs. Worst of all was the boredom of having nothing to do. Children and teenagers tried to keep busy with school, crafts, and sports. Some adults ran small businesses or coffeehouses. Others used skills they had learned in their native country, such as cutting hair or tailoring.

But the refugees spent most of their time in the camp waiting—waiting for the day when all of the papers necessary for immigration would be completed. "We were in Thailand for three years," Gu Thanh says. "It felt like a jail."

Many things can slow down the immigration process. When a family like the Huynhs applies to move to the United States, an agent from the U.S. Immigration and Naturalization Service (INS) opens a file of information about the family. The file includes documents such as birth certificates and military records. Sometimes documents must be sent from Vietnam, which can take a long time. The waiting period also depends on the number of people who have applied to immigrate, the number of available immigration officers, and the time it takes to process the applications.

Opposite: Refugees do construction work at a camp. *Below:* Many forms must be filled out to apply for immigration to the United States.

With their papers in hand, these refugees are ready to leave the camp.

The number of immigrants and refugees accepted into the United States varies year by year as immigration laws change. In 1988, for example, a total of 643,000 immigrants settled in the United States. Of these, 264,000 were from Asian countries, and 29,000 came from Vietnam.

Finally the day arrived when the papers for Gu Thanh and his family were ready. An INS agent interviewed them. After they were accepted as refugees, the INS arranged for them to travel to the United States, where their sponsors were waiting.

The Huynhs were lucky. They had family members who could pick them up at the airport, and they had a warm home to go to —the small, white stucco house in San Diego where KimHong's parents live.

For KimHong, the reunion with her mother and father and other members of her family made the hard journey to the United States worth it. Nonetheless, immigrating was a mixed blessing for both her and her husband, Gu Thanh.

"We have a proverb in Vietnam," Gu Thanh says. " 'No place is better than my country.' I am happy to be here, and I don't worry about anything anymore, but I still have my parents, brothers, and sister in Vietnam. I miss them so much."

KimHong's father works in the garden.

KimHong also has mixed feelings about the move. "In Vietnam, we lived under the Communist regime, so it was very difficult to get a job, hard to make money, and my children could not attend school," she reflects. "I like living in the United States with my family, but I think that if my country had not had the Communist regime, life would have been better there."

KimHong misses her native land. "I miss the fields," she says softly. She remembers the way they looked just after the monsoon season, with colored leaves falling from the trees, and the way the sun rose over the mountains. She does not like what Vietnam has become under Communist rule, but it is still her country, and she misses it—especially the Vietnam she knew as a girl.

Gu Thanh pauses to consider what his family has accomplished since leaving Vietnam. "We won," he says. "Now I think to myself, it was a terrible past. I want to forget everything that happened. I feel happy in this new country." He adds, "When you had a lot of things to survive, you do the best you can and you realize the value of life."

After breakfast Dan Thuy returns to her grandparents' house, where she joins her grandfather in front of the television. One of her favorite new pastimes is to watch Chinese movies on video. She also enjoys some of Southern California's special attractions.

"I like to go to Disneyland, the beach, and picnics with my parents," Dan Thuy says. "But then I think about my friends in Vietnam and I miss them so much."

In the afternoon, Dan Thuy, her mother, and Dan Tram help their aunt and cousins unload groceries from the car. They carry in bags of fresh vegetables and meats, which they will use to make Vietnamese rice and noodle soup with fish and pork. Later, Dan Thuy and KimHong slice the cooked pork and skim off the fat that has risen to the top of the large pot of broth. There is enough soup to feed the many family members and friends who will come and go all day and evening. Most Vietnamese families are extended ones that include aunts, uncles, cousins, and grandparents.

Dan Thuy is now beginning to feel at home in the United States. During her first days here, however, she was afraid. "I had trouble sleeping because the time wasn't the same, and everything I saw was different from my life in Thailand and Vietnam."

When Dan Thuy and her family arrived in San Diego, they needed help with communicating, grocery shopping, finding work, and enrolling in school. They had to learn how to open a bank account, how to use public transportation, and how to find their way around a strange city. Dan Thuy also encountered many unfamiliar items, such as a tube of toothpaste, a can opener, and a tape dispenser.

Immigrant children are often given a lot of responsibility in the new country. Because they usually learn the language faster than their parents, they are expected to act as translators—making doctor's appointments, answering the telephone, writing letters, and helping the adults read printed announcements, forms, and newspapers.

The challenges are less frightening for Dan Thuy now because she knows more English. Still, she is cautious. "I never go shopping alone," says Dan Thuy, "because I am afraid I would get lost."

Dan Thuy tastes the lemonade to see if it's ready.

Some things remain the same for the sisters. Dan Thuy and Dan Tram speak Vietnamese with their family. They see their parents and many Vietnamese cousins and friends each day. And they carry on their native traditions by helping with housekeeping and cooking. Girls in Vietnam usually help around the house more than most kids in the United States.

One custom they still enjoy is making fresh lemonade, Vietnamese style. Dan Thuy prepares the drink by soaking dozens of fresh lemons in a large bucket of water in the backyard. After two to three weeks, the mixture is ready to be sweetened with sugar and served.

Young immigrants may pay a high price to fit into American society. The clothes, cars, computers, movies, games, and toys typical of life in the United States are often in conflict with the values of other cultures. In Vietnam, for example, family loyalty and closeness are valued more than material possessions.

A common saying among many Southeast Asians emphasizes the importance of family unity: "To be with family is to be happy. To be without family is to be lost." Being together is more important than being alone. Children share rooms and extended families often share a house. If one member of the family needs money for food or clothing or transportation, other members share what they have. The privacy and independence that many Americans value so highly are not so important to the Vietnamese.

Dan Thuy's sister, Dan Tram, feels pulled between the old country and the new land. "When I lived in Vietnam, I wished I lived in the United States. But when I came here I wished I could go back to Vietnam to see my friends and my other grandparents." She wishes her father's parents lived in America, but she knows it may be many years before she sees them again.

In some ways, it can be more difficult for immigrant children to adjust to a new culture than it is for adults. Older people will not likely forget their native language and the customs that are part of their heritage. But children and teenagers are constantly pulled in different directions. They must speak English at school in order to survive and get ahead. Yet at home they are usually expected to converse in their native language. For young people who are still forming a sense of identity, hanging on to the native traditions can be a struggle.

Female immigrants may feel an even stronger sense of conflict than males. If their native culture does not value higher education for women or approve of women working outside the home, female immigrants might feel guilty if they attend college or want greater independence.

Dan Thuy follows the Vietnamese custom for women by learning to cook and keep house, but she is also excited about the opportunities available to American women. She wants to go to college to learn a skill she can use in a job. Her parents encourage her plans. One reason they left Vietnam was to provide a better life for their daughters, including a chance for a good education.

Since Dan Thuy's father cannot work now because of his back trouble, her mother must hold a job. "In Vietnam the wife usually stays home to take care of her family," KimHong explains. But she says she loves working, because she can earn money and improve her English. She is very busy now, since she works at the manicure shop every day and also helps her aging parents at home.

"My husband helps with a little of the housework," she says, "but he doesn't have to do too much because my mother and my daughters help."

KimHong is careful about allowing her daughters to be influenced too quickly by American customs. "I love the freedom here," she explains, "but I am also scared that too much freedom may cause the children to be bad."

More than anything, KimHong and Gu Thanh hope for a happy and peaceful future for their children. "I want my kids to have a good life here," says KimHong, "and to have the best education, but I also hope they never forget their homeland."

The next morning, Dan Thuy is off to Horace Mann Junior High School, which is a couple of miles from home. She looks forward to her favorite classes: P.E., English, and computer science. When she is not in the classroom, she plays volleyball with friends or eats lunch in the school cafeteria. She likes fried chicken and hamburgers best.

Like many immigrant teenagers, Dan Thuy is learning English through a process called "total immersion." That means she attends regular classes with the other students, practicing her English by listening and speaking in a variety of situations. She got an introduction to the language at the refugee camp, but there is still more to learn.

To increase her vocabulary, Dan Thuy goes to the school library and reads books in English. She also learns about her own culture at the public library. In an effort to serve the local immigrant population, one library in San Diego has enlarged its collection of Vietnamese books, information, and services. The Vietnamese materials include folklore, romance novels, information about United States citizenship, and instruction in English. (The Huynhs are not yet U.S. citizens. That will take about five years.)

Dan Thuy works at her desk at school.

Many inner-city schools in San Diego serve a large number of immigrants from Vietnam, Laos, Kampuchea, and China. Teachers at these schools make a point of incorporating Southeast Asian studies, festivals, and customs into their lesson plans.

Dan Thuy loves school. "I have a lot of friends there," she says, "and I like learning so much English."

Dan Tram, who is in fifth grade, is also adjusting quickly to her new life. One of the things Dan Tram likes best about America is the blend of cultures. "My wish is that I will have friends of many different countries," she says, "so that I can learn something good from each one of them." She adds, "My two new friends are Laotian and Mexican."

After school Dan Thuy helps her grandmother prepare dinner and do the laundry. Then she and Dan Tram talk with their family after dinner. "I like to tell my parents about different things that are happening in my life," says Dan Thuy. "I tell them about school and about my friends."

Later, following homework and some television, the sisters get ready for bed. Their bedroom looks like any American teenager's room: stuffed animals are piled on the beds and large posters of singers and movie stars hang on the wall.

Dan Thuy's grandmother gets ready to make dinner.

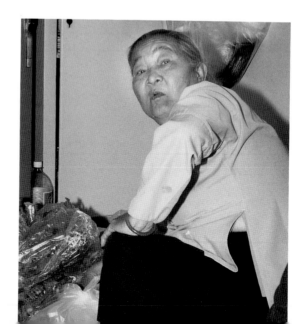

Dan Thuy holds a small doll that wears one of the hand-crocheted dresses she learned to make in the refugee camp. "I don't have time to crochet anymore," she says. She is too busy with school, sports, and friends.

"My dream is to continue studying and to attend college," she says. Before climbing into her bunk bed, Dan Thuy writes a letter to her grandparents in Vietnam, telling them about her new life in the United States.

For Further Reading

Ashabranner, Brent, and Melissa Ashabranner. *Into a Strange Land: Unaccompanied Refugee Youth in America.* New York: Dodd, Mead & Co., 1987.

Bode, Janet. *New Kids on the Block: Oral Histories of Immigrant Teens.* New York: Franklin Watts, 1989.

Brown, Tricia. *Lee Ann: The Story of a Vietnamese Girl.* New York: G.P. Putnam's Sons, 1991.

Dolan, Edward F. *America After Vietnam: Legacies of a Hated War.* New York: Franklin Watts, 1989.

Goldfarb, Mace, M.D. *Fighters, Refugees, Immigrants: A Story of the Hmong.* Minneapolis: Carolrhoda Books, 1982.

Haskins, James. *The New Americans: Vietnamese Boat People.* Hillside, N.J.: Enslow Pub., 1980.

Rutledge, Paul. *The Vietnamese in America.* Minneapolis: Lerner Pub., 1987.